THE ROYAL SHAKESPEARE COMPANY

The Royal Shakespeare Company is probably one of the best-known theatre companies in the world. It has operated in its present form since 1961 when it changed its name from the Shakespeare Memorial Theatre Company, established a London base and widened its repertoire to embrace works other than Shakespeare.

Today the RSC has five home theatres. In Stratford the Royal Shakespeare Theatre stages large-scale productions of Shakespeare's plays; the Swan, a galleried Jacobean playhouse, brings to light the plays of many of his neglected contemporaries alongside classics of world theatre, while The Other Place, the company's studio theatre, houses some of the company's most exciting experimental and contemporary work, as well as providing a regular venue for visiting companies and some of the RSC's education work, including the annual Prince of Wales Shakespeare School.

In 1982 the company moved its London home to the Barbican Centre, where in the large-scale Barbican Theatre and the studio-sized Pit Theatre, the company stages new productions as well as the repertoire transferring from Stratford.

But Stratford and London are only part of the story. Recent years have seen a dramatic increase in the reach of the RSC, with major RSC productions on tour around the UK and abroad. Productions from Stratford and London visit regional theatres, while our annual regional tour continues to set up its own travelling auditorium in schools and community centres around the country. This ensures that the RSC's productions are available to the widest possible number of people geographically. An extensive programme of education work accompanies all this, creating the audiences of tomorrow by bringing the excitement and the power of theatre to young people all over the country. Between November 2000 and June 2001 the RSC will have presented over 40 weeks of theatre in more than 25 towns and cities in the UK, outside our own theatres.

In the past few years the company has taken Shakespeare to enthusiastic audiences in Europe, the USA, Australia and New Zealand, South America, Japan, India and Pakistan, Hong Kong, Turkey and Korea. The RSC is grateful to The British Council for its support of its overseas touring programme.

Despite enormous changes over the _____ ion very much as an ensemble of actors and _____ ith those of the world's top directors and des _____ teams to give a distinctive and unmistakable approach to _____

THE ROYAL SHAKESPEARE COMPANY

RSC EDUCATION

The objective of the RSC Education Department is to enable as many people as possible from all walks of life to have easy access to the great works of Shakespeare, the Renaissance and the theatre.

To do this, we are building a team which supports the productions that the company presents onstage for the general public, special interest groups and for education establishments of all kinds.

We are also planning to develop our contribution as a significant learning resource in the fields of Shakespeare, the Renaissance, classical and modern theatre, theatre arts and the RSC. This resource is made available in many different ways, including workshops, teachers' programmes, summer courses, a menu of activities offered to group members of the audience, pre- and post-show events as part of the Events programme, open days, tours of the theatre, community activities, youth programmes and loans of parts of the RSC Collection for exhibitions.

We are building, for use worldwide, a new web site to be launched this year. This will make available all of the above, as well as providing access to the RSC's collection of historic theatre and Shakespearean material. It will also carry interesting and interactive material about the work of the RSC.

We can also use our knowledge of theatre techniques to help in other aspects of learning: classroom teaching techniques for subjects other than drama or English, including management and personnel issues.

Not all of these programmes are available all the time, and not all of them are yet in place. However, if you are interested in pursuing any of these options, or for information on general education activities, contact Education Administrator Sarah Keevill on 01789 403462, or e-mail her on sarah.keevill@ rsc.org.uk.

JOIN THE RSC

For £8 a year you can become an RSC Associate Member. Benefits include:
* Advance Information and priority booking for our Stratford and London seasons (plus the RSC Residency if you live in the appropriate area).
* Special priority booking subscription scheme for the Stratford Summer Festival Season.
* Deferred payment facilities on Stratford tickets booked during the priority period (by instalments with a credit card).
* Special Members' performances for some Stratford and London productions.
* No fees payable on ticket re-sales in Stratford.
* Free RSC Magazine

Full members
For £24 all of the Associate benefits, plus:
* Guaranteed seats for RSC productions in the Royal Shakespeare Theatre, Swan Theatre and Barbican Theatre (for tickets booked during the priority period).
* An extra week of priority booking for Stratford and London seasons.
* 10% discount on purchases from RSC Shops.

Group and **Education** membership also available.

Overseas Members
The RSC tours regularly overseas. In recent years we've visited the USA, South America, Japan, India and Pakistan, as well as most parts of Europe. Wherever you are in the world, you can become an RSC Member. Overseas Membership is available from £15.

Special Overseas Members
All the benefits of a Full Member, plus:
* A complimentary programme for each Royal Shakespeare Theatre production.

For further information write to the Membership Office, Royal Shakespeare Theatre, Stratford-upon-Avon, CV37 6BB or telephone 01789 403440.

STAY IN TOUCH
For up-to-date news on the RSC, our productions and education work, visit the RSC's official web site: **www.rsc.org.uk**. Information on RSC performances is also available on Teletext.

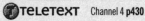 Channel 4 **p430**

A PARTNERSHIP WITH THE RSC

The RSC is immensely grateful for the valuable support of its corporate sponsors and individual and charitable donors. Between them these groups provide up to £6m a year for the RSC and support a range of initiatives such as actor training, education workshops and access to our performances for all members of society.

Among our corporate sponsors we are especially grateful to Allied Domecq, principal sponsor since 1994, for its far-sighted and long-standing relationship. Allied Domecq's announcement that its principal sponsorship will come to a natural end in 2001 provides an exciting opportunity for companies to form new corporate partnerships with the RSC, as principal sponsor, as a member of the RSC's new Business Partners programme or as a corporate member.

As an individual you may wish to support the work of the RSC through membership of the RSC Patrons. For as little as £21 per month you can join a cast drawn from our audience and the worlds of theatre, film, politics and business. Alternatively, the gift of a legacy to the RSC would enable the company to maintain and increase new artistic and educational work with children and adults through the Acting and Education Funds.

For information about corporate partnership with the RSC, please contact:
Liam Fisher-Jones
Director of Development
Barbican Theatre
London EC2Y 8BQ
Tel: 020 7382 7132
E-mail: liamfj@rsc.org.uk

For information about individual relationships with the RSC, please contact:
Graeme Williamson
Development Manager
Royal Shakespeare Theatre
Waterside, Stratford-upon-Avon CV37 6BB.
Tel: 01789 412661
E-mail: graemew@rsc.org.uk

You can visit our web site at **www.rsc.org.uk/development**

Loveplay was first performed by the Royal Shakespeare Company
in the Pit Theatre, London, on 28 February 2001.
The cast was as follows:

Simon Coates	Herek/Trevelyn/Mr Quilley/Buttermere/Dieter
Ian Dunn	Marcus/Deric/Man/De Vere/Gwyn/Peter
Niamh Linehan	Woman/Matilda/Roxanne/Lynne/Brigitta
Alison Newman	Dorcas/Hilda/Marianne/Miss Tilly/Joy/Anita
Neil Warhurst	Eric/Llewellyn/Boy/Quinn
Jody Watson	Gilda/Helen/Millie/Flynn/Rita

Directed by	**Anthony Clark**
Designed by	**Rachel Blues**
Lighting designed by	**Richard Beaton**
Music by	**Conor Linehan**
Fights by	**Malcolm Ranson**
Sound by	**Steff Langley**
Assistant Director	**Emma Wolukau-Wanambwa**
Company voice work by	**David Willis and Andrew Wade**
Dialect work by	**Neil Swain**
Production Manager	**Patrick Frazer**
Costume Supervisor	**Jane Dickerson**

Stage Manager	**Michael Budmani/Paul Sawtell**
Deputy Stage Manager	**Paul Sawtell/Stephen Cressy**
Assistant Stage Manager	**Robin Longley**

time, periods, love, history

__Keening__ rhyming names?

Enlightenment time p. 47

point of Romantic story?

Empire love & evil

'60s freedom p. 68

who is Flynn?

Loveplay

Moira Buffini won a *Time Out* award for her performance
in *Jordan*, which she co-wrote with Anna Reynolds.
It won the Writers' Guild Award for Best Fringe Play
in 1992. Since then she has written *Blavatsky's Tower*
(*Time Out* Critics' Choice at the Machine Room, 1998),
Gabriel for Soho Theatre (winner of the LWT Plays on
Stage Award and Meyer-Whitworth Award, 1997) and
Silence for the National Theatre Studio and Birmingham
Rep (winner of the Susan Smith Blackburn Prize and
TMA Award nominee). She is currently under
commission to the National Theatre.

[handwritten notes:]

Sc. 4 pp. 30 – 41   Trevelyn   Brian
                     Helen   ~~Stafford~~ Mo
                     Llewellyn   Joe

pp 76 – 90   Rita   Sono
              Anita   Michele
              Dieter   Lucas
              Brigitta ~~Nina~~ Jean
              Peter   ~~Patrick~~
                       Aaron

MOIRA BUFFINI

Loveplay

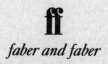

faber and faber

First published in 2001
by Faber and Faber Limited
3 Queen Square, London WC1N 3AU
Published in the United States by Faber and Faber Inc.
an affiliate of Farrar, Straus and Giroux LLC, New York

Typeset by Country Setting, Kingsdown, Kent CT14 8ES
Printed in England by Mackays of Chatham plc, Chatham, Kent

A CIP record for this book
is available from the British Library

ISBN 0-571-20983-1

2 4 6 8 10 9 7 5 3 1

For Martin

Loveplay was first performed by the Royal Shakespeare Company in the Pit Theatre, London, on 28 February 2001. The cast was as follows:

Herek/Trevelyn/Mr Quilley/Buttermere/Dieter
  Simon Coates
Marcus/Deric/Man/De Vere/Gwyn/Peter Ian Dunn
Woman/Matilda/Roxanne/Lynne/Brigitta
  Niamh Linehan
Eric/Llewellyn/Boy/Quinn Neil Warhurst
Dorcas/Hilda/Marianne/Miss Tilly/Joy/Anita
  Alison Newman
Gilda/Helen/Nillie/Flynn/Rita Jody Watson

Directed by Anthony Clark
Designed by Rachel Blues
Lighting designed by Richard Beaton
Music by Conor Linehan
Fights by Malcolm Ranson
Sound by Steff Langley

Characters

Marcus, a Roman
Dorcas, a businesswoman

Herek, a Saxon
Eric, a Saxon
Deric, a Saxon
Woman

Gilda, a novice
Hilda, a rebel
Matilda, a nun

Trevelyn, an actor
Llewellyn, a playwright
Helen, a malcontent

Roxanne, a scientist
Marianne, a servant
Man, an artisan

Miss Tilly, a governess
Mr Quilley, her employer
Millie, his wife

De Vere, an artist
Buttermere, a vicar

Joy, a prostitute
Boy, a virgin

Quinn, a revolutionary
Flynn, a convert
Gwyn, an adventurer
Lynne, an adventurer

Brigitta, a single woman
Anita, a matchmaker
Rita, a secretary
Dieter, an alcoholic
Peter, a doctor

The action takes place on the same small square of land, which moves through time from the past to the present.

The title of each scene should be shown.

The play can be performed with as few as six actors.

LOVEPLAY

Scene One

THE CLASSICAL AGE

AD 79. *Open land. A half-built structure of wood and stone. Dorcas runs on. She lifts her skirts at someone following her, laughs and runs off. Marcus, a Roman soldier, enters in pursuit. He exits. We hear Dorcas shrieking and giggling. Marcus enters, pulling her by the arm.*

Marcus (*pulling Dorcas down*) Here. You. Now. This.

Dorcas Hang on; I got something in my back. (*She pushes something out from underneath her.*) What're you building here then? What's that?

Marcus Going to be latrines for the garrison.

Dorcas What's a latrine?

Marcus It's a structure of wood and stone, designed for us to shit in.

Dorcas You're building a building to shit in?

Marcus It's what we do. We have latrines.

Dorcas You can't shit in a building.

Marcus Why not?

Dorcas It's not natural. Why don't you shit in the woods like human beings?

Marcus Because we're civilised. Can we talk after?

Dorcas Don't have to talk at all if you like.

Marcus Great.

Dorcas Hang on. Isn't there something you're forgetting?

Marcus Oh yes, sorry. (*He gives her a coin.*) Here.

Dorcas (*looking at it blankly*) What's this?

Marcus A coin.

Dorcas What's a coin?

Marcus It's money. You can buy yourself something with it.

Dorcas (*uncomprehending*) What?

Marcus You can exchange this money for goods. Take it to market and buy something.

Dorcas I have to go all the way to market to get my payment?

Marcus No, that's your payment. You go to market to *spend* it.

Dorcas So all you're giving me is this?

Marcus (*trying to begin*) It's plenty; it's loads.

Dorcas (*stopping him*) It's usually a chicken.

Marcus Pardon?

Dorcas I usually get at least a chicken.

Marcus But that coin is worth more than a chicken.

Dorcas No it ain't.

Marcus In exchange for that coin you'd probably get a chicken, a bag of grain and some fruit. You might even get a piglet. Come on.

Dorcas I want a chicken.

Marcus I haven't got a chicken. I've got that. It's *money*.

Dorcas I don't wannit.

Dorcas drops the coin. She turns her face from Marcus. Pause.

Marcus Can I owe you a chicken?

Dorcas Do I look stupid?

Marcus Look, the coin means chicken. Take it to a vendor of chickens and he'll say: 'That is *currency*. I accept it. Here is a large chicken.'

Dorcas No one in their right mind would swap a chicken for that.

Marcus Not swap! It's *legal tender*, an entire system, the basis for the whole structure of civilised – Look, please . . . I've been on the road for weeks. I'm aching for this.

Dorcas Aching?

Marcus Yes . . .

Dorcas (*sympathetically*) Ahhh . . . (*She feels his cloak.*) Tell you what; this is nice. Isn't it soft?

Marcus My cloak?

Dorcas You can gimme that, if you like.

Marcus You can't have my cloak.

Dorcas Why not?

Marcus It's regulation issue. You only get one, and if you lose it you freeze. It's bloody cold here.

Dorcas It's a lovely colour.

Marcus Thanks.

Dorcas What d'you call that fabric then?

Marcus Wool.

Dorcas Wool? Really?

Marcus I think so.

Dorcas It's a fabulous weave. How did they get it like that?

Marcus I don't know. Look –

Dorcas Do you have different sheep down there in Rome or something?

Marcus You can't have it.

Dorcas Go on.

Marcus No! . . . Frankly, it's worth more than we agreed on.

Dorcas More than a chicken?

Marcus Yes.

Dorcas You're saying it's worth more than me.

Marcus I'm saying it would be foolish of me to give up my cloak for one shag.

Dorcas Two shags. One now and one later.

Marcus No!

Dorcas Right. (*shoving him off*) Off you get.

Marcus Look. You're lucky I'm offering to pay you at all. I could just take you.

Dorcas Oh, could you?

Marcus (*becoming violent*) Right now!

Dorcas Take me and I BITE! If you enter me without my will, the pain of it will make you think you dipped it in poison. Never again will you use it for pleasure. You'll piss acid; desire will eat away at you with no release! It won't be the first time I've used this power. British women are like mouths down there, with teeth: force us and we will make you shrink. You're shrivelling now; I can feel it. Like a slug on salt.

Marcus (*getting up*) Right. Forget it.

Dorcas Oh, have I upset you? I'm so sorry. Come on, Roman, show us the might of your empire. You're very welcome if you just give me a chicken or your cloak.

Marcus spits on her. She laughs.

Dorcas Scared you, have I?

Marcus We will crush you. You will fall under the foundations of our city like dust. When we've finished here, creatures like you won't exist! (*Marcus exits.*)

Dorcas 'Course we will. Creatures like me will always exist. (*Dorcas picks up the coin. She examines it.*) Money. (*She throws the coin into the air and catches it.*) Money for nothing.

Scene Two

THE DARK AGE

544. The space has become a clearing in a wood. The Roman latrines are in ruins. The grunts of a man having sex can be heard from within. Two grimy Saxons, Eric and Herek, are sitting in front, at a fire.

Eric What d'you reckon it was, that place?

Herek (*looking behind him*) Some sort o' temple, I s'pose. Can't see why they'd build anything else out of stone. It's got a shelf of wood. About that high. Big, round holes in it. An altar, I reckon. I threw her down on it but it was rotted. She went right through. (*Pause.*) Did it on the floor in the end.

Eric I don't like the idea of doing it in a temple.

Herek Why not? It's not a temple any more, is it? It's nothing now.

Eric What about their gods?

Herek Their gods are dead, aren't they? Dead, along with all o' them. That city we walked through back there; ruins tall as trees and not a sod in sight. A dead nation. Hundreds of years' worth of dead.

Eric What makes you think their gods are dead?

Herek Well, they must be. They're no longer worshipped.

Eric A god is immortal. The presence of a god endures, 'specially in a sacred place, even when his name is long forgot.

18

Herek Well . . .

Eric I'm not doing it in there.

Herek Why not?

Eric I might invoke a curse.

Herek Look, I done it in there and I'm fine.

Eric How do you know?

Herek Cause my dick hasn't fallen off.

Eric Yet.

Herek Look, if you don't wanna do it in the hut, do it in the woods.

Eric I'll do it here. By the light.

Herek Not in front of me you won't. Take her in the woods like a human being.

Eric I'll do it here.

Herek Why?

Eric I don't like the woods. A wood has spirits.

Herek Fuck's sake.

Eric Didn't you feel them as we brought her through? The same eyes that were watching us in that city were watching us in the wood.

    The grunts are reaching a crescendo.

Herek It's always something with you, isn't it? Eyes, spirits, omens – always some fucking thing looking at you.

Eric The eyes of the dead.

Herek Oh, please.

Eric They don't like us.

Herek Eric . . .

Eric I've been on my guard against them all day long. I can feel them, here, in this place. They want to suck our lives out.

They pause uncomfortably while the man in the ruin comes to a climax.

Herek Eric, can I tell you something, for the sake of your own, you know, sanity?

Eric What?

Herek The dead are dead; finish. And this place is just a place.

Eric A place is never just a place. Everywhere you go, you have a crux – like a joining – of time, flesh, spirit – of *stuff*; past events, future portents all crowding in, visible only to the mind. It causes pressure.

Herek Well, if you don't like it here, maybe we should go. Let's just go.

Eric What about my release?

Herek What about it?

Eric I want it and I'm having it here, by the light. How can I have peace until I've had my release?

Herek You find peace in it, do you? In a rape, you find peace?

Eric Rape or not rape; makes no difference. Power, then peace . . . Why, what do you find?

Herek I don't look for anything. I just do it.

Deric (*entering from the hut*) All yours, mate.

Eric Bring her out here.

Deric What for?

Eric I want her out here.

Deric She's in there.

Herek He doesn't like the hut.

Deric What's wrong with it?

Eric Bring her out!

Deric Fuck's sake . . . (*He exits.*)

Herek You should calm down, Eric. All this shit about spirits and dead gods; it fucks you up. As if there's some great meaning to everything we're doing, as if some higher power cares. It's pathetic really, 'cause there is no higher power, there is nothing apart from this – what we do and what we see. That is the meaning. To exist here, now, and follow every desire we have. Like if I want to eat, I eat. If I want a shit, I have one. If I want to shag, I find something to shag and I shag it. That's it. As soon as something's happened, it's gone, dead, over – and as to things that haven't happened yet, as to the future, as to omens and portents and curses; well it's such a lot of shit I can't even bring myself to speak on the subject.

Eric You'll discover you're wrong when it's too late.

Deric enters with a Woman over his shoulder.

Deric Shall I dump her in the woods, then?

Eric Here.

Deric What, right here?

Eric By the light.

Deric You're not expecting us to watch, are you?

Eric You can do what you like.

Deric I'm not watching.

Eric Then go elsewhere.

Herek Oh, let him get on with it. It'll only take five seconds anyway.

Deric I don't believe it . . .

> *Deric dumps the Woman by Eric and stands as far apart as he can. Herek joins him. Eric prepares himself by praying.*

You see, there's something about doing it which is fine, and something about watching some other bloke do it which is not fine – know what I mean?

Herek I know exactly what you mean.

Deric (*intimately*) Because it's not about watching or looking at all, is it? The whole thing. It's about . . . I mean, even having your eyes open is not a good idea. There was one point, when I had my eyes open right, and this, between you and me – I mean strictly – is why it took me a while to finish. 'Cause I could see that she was looking at me. I could see her eyes in the dark like . . . like marsh lights shining out of her skull, you know? And her face in some kind of . . . contortion. And I thought, shall I hit her and blot it out? But I'd already hit her pretty hard, so I just thought no, I'll close my eyes. So I shut 'em and I thought of nothing, and then, at last, I found myself in that place which is the favourite place of all men since the world began.

> *Herek sniggers.*

Deric Not that place! – I was already there! I'm talking about the, the *place* inside you that opens up – the . . . the mind. More than the mind . . . the, the spirit, the –

Herek Self.

Deric The being, yeh. Am I making sense?

Herek Yep.

Deric When I'm doing it, I am most myself –

Herek Right.

Deric I am most fully me –

Herek Yeh.

Deric In that place of closed eyes and darkness –

Herek Right.

Deric Of boundless freedom and – and limitless . . .

Herek Present.

Deric Yeh, the mysterious – I don't know –

Herek Moment of self.

Deric Timeless . . . Time disappears, don't it. And for that moment, you are everything, everywhere. You are Beyond.

Eric (*examining the Woman*) Deric, would you come here for a moment, please?

Deric What?

Eric Could you tell me what I'm supposed to do with this?

   Deric and Herek approach Eric.

Eric Should I bury it, or burn it?

Deric What d'you mean? (*He lifts the Woman and lets her drop.*)

Eric It's dead.

Deric No, she just fainted, mate.

23

Eric Look at it.

Deric She ain't dead.

Eric It's nothing but a thing. Dead!

Deric She can't be dead.

Eric (*furious*) You careless fucking bastard! What about my release?

Deric Look, I only hit her. There's no way she's dead; she was looking at me!

Eric (*backing away*) There's no release in that, no power to be gained from it, nothing. I'm not touching it. It's gone.

Deric You mean, while I was – She was –

Eric The gods have taken her, not you! (*He turns towards the hut.*) I haven't set foot in it! I haven't defiled it! Whatever god you are, LEAVE ME BE! (*Eric runs off.*)

Deric What's he talking about? What god?

Herek He gives me the fucking jitters, that bloke. (*He gathers his things.*) Get your stuff. We're going.

Deric What god?

Herek He thinks that some great supernatural force actually cares about what we've done here. It's dogshit.

He follows Eric. Deric stares at the Woman. The darkness grows.

Deric You shouldn't of looked at me.

He goes. At last the Woman stirs. She slowly gets to her knees. She retches. She stands. She wails. A kind of keening. The sound of anguish – and rage. It is replaced by . . .

Scene Three

THE NEW MILLENNIUM

1099. Gilda, a novice, singing. Eerie, otherworldly, ecstatic. The space has become an abbey. Hilda watches Gilda, moved. She approaches her. Gilda sings, oblivious.

Hilda Sister . . .

Gilda stops singing. She smiles. Hilda suddenly turns away and points towards a wall.

Sister, look!

Gilda What? Where?

Hilda There . . .

Gilda What?

Hilda Can't you see?

Gilda Where?

Hilda Him!

Gilda Who?

Hilda falls to her knees.

I can't see anything!

Matilda enters. She watches the others, unseen.

Don't lie to me; there's nothing there . . .

Hilda He's standing quite still, his hand stretched out as if he wants something.

Gilda What?

Hilda I think you've drawn him with your singing . . .

Gilda Oh!

Hilda You must be able to see him!

Gilda Oh! . . . Oh, I can't breathe! What is he?

Hilda I don't know.

Gilda I've had dreams about the spirit of this place.

Hilda Yes.

Gilda Is it him?

Hilda He's gazing at you.

Gilda Oh, I don't know what to do! Why can't I see?

Hilda Perhaps – I don't know – maybe he wants you to see him with your heart, not with your eyes. If you closed them –

Gilda (*closing them*) Yes –

Hilda You might see him.

Gilda I . . . (*She concentrates.*) Yes.

Hilda He's coming closer.

Gilda Barefoot!

Hilda Yes.

Gilda His eyes are so . . . Oh, he's going to –!

Hilda What?

Gilda He's holding out his arms to me . . .

Hilda He's speaking.

Gilda Yes . . .

Hilda He says that when you sing, he –

Gilda He wants to kiss my lips.

Hilda kisses Gilda. Gilda opens her eyes. She swipes Hilda, shocked, furious.

Hilda He was using me as his vessel.

Gilda spits the kiss away. She exits. Hilda is hurt. She tries to recover herself.

Matilda What on earth were you doing?

Hilda (*spinning round*) Nothing.

Matilda Conjuring spirits out of the air?

Hilda There was nothing there.

Matilda So you were trying to dupe her?

Hilda No.

Matilda Then what?

Hilda I love her.

Matilda No you don't.

Hilda I love all my sisters, like I'm supposed to.

Matilda You *want* her.

Hilda I love her.

Matilda You desire her. Can I tell you something about desire?

Hilda I don't think you know anything about it, do you?

Matilda Are you being rude to me?

Hilda You're going to throw me out –

Matilda Am I?

Hilda So what difference does it make / how I behave?

Matilda I'm trying to help you! You think I've never felt desire? When I first came here I was eaten up with it, just like you are. I was raging with it, seething. It's like a prison isn't it?

Hilda This place is a prison!

Matilda No, no, listen to me. I know you didn't choose this life; neither did I. I felt the way you do – so angry, torn from everything I longed for. I thought I was in chains. But what I found here was peace. This place is freedom . . .

Hilda Freedom?

Matilda Yes.

Hilda When we're locked inside these walls?

Matilda The walls need never confine you. I barely notice them; my mind has soared over them so many times. Sister, your spirit is the most precious thing you possess. It's lovelier and more lasting than the smoothness of your flesh. Our bodies are only an encumbrance and when we realise this, we let the spirit, our true beauty, fly. I have knelt on this floor and gone so far in thought, in inspiration, that I have felt the mystery of infinity within my grasp. Liberate your spirit and you could turn these walls into everywhere, you could make nothing of time itself. Let me show you. I can teach you. You only have to leave the physical, the animal, the flesh behind.

Hilda Why did you watch us? You could have made us stop. Why did you *watch*?

Matilda I was . . . observing / in order to –

Hilda Were you leeching my desire or hers?

Matilda I'm trying to help you.

Hilda No you're not.

Matilda You're in pain, a pain I recognise and I am trying to help!

Hilda You're trying to seduce me.

Matilda How dare you!

Hilda You want us joined, twined like bodiless lovers, so you can lead me . . . where? Towards peace? I call your peace cowardice. I call your life of spirit death.

Matilda No, flesh is death. Flesh is maggot-food. It's grave-fodder!

Hilda (*touches her*) Is that why you cringe from my touch? You haven't conquered your desire. You live in fear of it.

Matilda You'll spend the night in here like the fool that you are. On your knees. Find something that endures before it is too late.

Matilda goes to exit. She stays. She watches. Hilda closes her eyes. We hear an echo of Gilda singing.

Hilda Come back. Come back. Sing to me . . . I will think you back.

Helen enters (played by the same actress as Gilda). She spreads a cloak on the ground. She kneels on it, as the space becomes . . .

Scene Four

THE RENAISSANCE

*1584. A ruined abbey. Helen is joined by Trevelyn. He
takes her hand. Hilda looks on.*

Trevelyn
Angel.

Helen
        My love.

Trevelyn
                At last, tell me I may.

Helen
You may. You could before. Your noble strength
Alone has kept this woman's body frail
And slight, from that which always it desired.

Trevelyn kisses Helen's hand.

Why cease? These unpluck'd lips of mine
Are wasted in mere speech. You are my life
And soon as dawn ascends with light sublime,
I'll be your loving, ever faithful wife.

Trevelyn
But angel, wait –

Helen
             Why wait?

*Helen kisses Trevelyn full on the lips. Hilda exits.
Helen reaches for his body and pulls him towards her.
He breaks away, shocked at her passion.*

Trevelyn
                What is't you do?

Helen
What both of us desire.

Trevelyn
                              We can't, my love!
My dear betroth'd, my alabaster queen,
Forbear a few more hours. Our trusty priest
Arrives at dawn to join us; man and wife.
'Til then, inflame my loins no more –

Helen
                                        'Tis love
Alone that urges me; now kiss!

Trevelyn
                              O bride
Of virgin snow, believe me when I say
There is a difference great as dark and day
Between a lover's lawless, wanton kiss
And one God-given, sweet in nuptial bliss.

Helen
My kiss tonight is different from the morn?
But why, when both are freely, gladly borne?

Trevelyn
The difference lies not in the kiss alone
But in what you bestow and what I own.

Helen
I do not understand.

Trevelyn
                        Once man and wife –

Helen
You do not wish to kiss me!

Trevelyn
                              'Pon my life
I do, with lips as red as wine, but darling
Only wait, 'til I am yours and you are mine.

Enter Llewellyn, a malcontent.

Llewellyn (*aside*)
 I am a bastard. I have come
 In black and ruinous mood with festering mind
 To see what chaos and corruption I can find.
 Where I find none, in this sweet lovers' scene,
 I'll make my own, with sulphurous, sickly spleen.
 Llewellyn, jade of Fortune and her wheel,
 Will smash their love, like glass beneath his heel.
 For I, who watched this pockish mouse Trevelyn
 Woo the beauteous, amorous Lady Helen
 Am so pent up with envy that to see them wed
 Will send me green and frenzied to my bed.
 So here, amid the ruins of this place,
 Where brides of Christ once walked in lowly grace,
 Here, where ne'er a violent act was done,
 I've plotted rape and murder. I've begun –

Helen (*to Llewellyn*) Sorry, my love.

Llewellyn (*stopping, annoyed*) What?

Helen Forgive me but I'm not sure what we're supposed to be doing.

Llewellyn You're waiting for the priest.

Helen Yes. But while you're making your speech, what are we doing?

Llewellyn You're in a tableau of love.

Helen Oh. It's just that we're halfway through an argument, quite an important argument, and it seems a little strange that we should stop, that's all.

Llewellyn You stop because I make my entrance.

Helen Yes, but I'm asking my betrothed, the classics tutor I've given up everything for, why his perception of me will change after we're married – aren't I? Why he somehow finds it more desirable to kiss me as his wife than as his lover – and then we just stop, while you do your speech. Forgive me, but it doesn't make sense.

Llewellyn My speech is an 'aside'. I enter, I do an 'aside', and the action on stage stops.

Helen Yes, but –

Llewellyn It's called a convention. It makes perfect sense.

Helen But this kiss is never referred to again. And what does she think? Is she quite content that he doesn't want to kiss her? She's torn herself from her family and thrown away her wealth. She needs reassurance – and he won't kiss her!

Llewellyn Well?

Helen I think it might make her worry.

Llewellyn Worry what?

Helen That he's not the man she thought.

Pause. Llewellyn is shocked.

Trevelyn Look, to tell you the truth, my friend, I don't think it makes sense either.

Llewellyn Excellent.

Trevelyn You see, my problem is, why is he saying it in the first place? You've got to admit it's rather insipid. I mean here they are, two lovers, alone in the moonlit ruins of an ancient abbey – and any average, hot-blooded fellow would just . . . kiss her.

Llewellyn Yes, but he's nobler than that. We have to get the contrast between him and the villain. He wants to kiss her, more than anything – but he restrains himself.

Trevelyn Why?

Llewellyn Because his intentions are impeccable. He's seeking to ennoble their love by the example of his virtue. By not kissing her, we can see that he's worthy of her, that he's upright, pure in heart!

Trevelyn I don't think the audience will get that. He just comes over as a sissy milksop. And, er – that's not what I play.

Llewellyn Fine.

Trevelyn I play the hero. I'm an expert in heroes; I've been playing them since my voice broke and I can tell you, my friend, the hero would kiss her.

Llewellyn Well. You'd better kiss her then. (*He turns away.*)

Helen My dearest love . . . nobody meant to offend you. We were just saying –

Llewellyn No, no, no, you're right. It doesn't make sense. Erase it.

Trevelyn What?

Llewellyn Erase the whole scene. Forget it existed.

Helen We're not saying –

Llewellyn Yes you are! It doesn't work and that's fine. It's what we've come here to find out; to play the scene in its real environment – a ruined abbey by moonlight – to see if it works. It clearly doesn't. So. Scrub out the lines from where Lady Helen says 'I'll be your loving, ever faithful wife' all the way down to my entrance.

Helen So . . . what are we doing when you come in, my love?

Llewellyn You're kissing him.

Helen Right.

Llewellyn Like you wanted to.

Helen (*pause*) What do you mean by that?

Llewellyn I mean I can sense the general feeling. And there's no point opposing the general *feeling*, is there? They're only lines, after all. When I wrote them I thought they had some power and beauty, some universal truth, but now I see I was wrong.

Helen You asked us to say what we thought.

Llewellyn Throw them away! They're ephemeral. (*bitterly*) Like love. (*He goes to the entrance and turns.*) Right. From the start. (*to Trevelyn*) This time, when I enter, you're giving her a big, hot-blooded, manly kiss.

Llewellyn exits. Helen and Trevelyn arrange themselves for the opening of the scene.

Trevelyn Well, sorry, but if it doesn't work, it doesn't work.

Helen We've hurt him.

Trevelyn He shouldn't be so sensitive. Like he says, they're only lines – and between you and me, they're not very good.

Helen It's autobiographical.

Trevelyn What?

Helen This scene. It's about us. He was my tutor in classics and philosophy. He told me about his struggles to be a poet and his plight opened my heart. He said I was his only muse. He used to write sonnets and push them into my hand as I conjugated verbs. It was so *forbidden* . . . I thought he had a perfect understanding of love but –

Trevelyn (*amazed*) Helen . . .

Helen – the night before I married him, when we ran away from my father's, we got lost on the road. I wanted to kiss him, well, more than kiss him, and he pushed me away, literally held me at arm's length.

Trevelyn How could he?

Helen He was being noble. I think.

Trevelyn My God . . . I've just called him a sissy.

Llewellyn (*off*) What are we waiting for?

Trevelyn Yes. (*Shouts.*) Just seen another problem, my friend!

Llewellyn (*enters, visibly frustrated*) What?

Trevelyn Well, your lovely wife is rehearsing the part because you wanted everything to be real, which is a marvellous idea, really innovative – but when we return to the theatre, she'll be back in the purgatory of wardrobe and I'll have to kiss a little, adolescent boy. With onion breath, probably. Right the way through your speech.

Llewellyn Well?

Trevelyn I don't like the idea.

Llewellyn (*with controlled impatience*) Are you an actor?

Trevelyn Yes, I am an actor.

Llewellyn Then act.

He exits. Trevelyn smarts under the insult. He takes Helen's hand.

Trevelyn You sacrificed wealth and family for him?

Helen (*with great sadness*) I would have sacrificed anything.

Trevelyn
　Angel.

Helen
　　　My love.

Trevelyn
　　　　At last, tell me I may.

Helen
　You may. You could before. Your noble strength
　Alone has kept this woman's body frail
　And slight, from that which always it desired.

　Trevelyn kisses her hand.

　Why cease? These unpluck'd lips of mine
　Are wasted in mere speech. You are my life
　And soon as dawn ascends with light sublime,
　I'll be your loving, ever faithful –

　*They kiss. It's overpowering. The passion of it takes
　them both aback. It continues while:*

Llewellyn (*enters, aside*)
　I am a bastard. I have come
　In black and ruinous mood, with festering mind
　To see what chaos and corruption I can find.
　Where I find none, in this sweet lovers' scene,
　I'll make my own, with sulphurous, sickly spleen.
　Llewellyn, jade of Fortune and her wheel,
　Will smash their love, like glass beneath his heel.
　For I, who watched the pockish mouse Trevelyn
　Woo the passionate, amorous Lady Helen
　Am so pent up –

　*His glance falls upon Helen and Trevelyn. He falters.
　Helen and Trevelyn continue to kiss for just a moment
　too long. They part.*

Trevelyn Is something wrong? We were acting. Like you said. You said act, and we acted.

Llewellyn It's a strange place, this ruin, don't you think? Built by ancient hands and stuffed with the plunder of ages. And now . . . five hundred years of holy history, gone. Generations of clasped hands, rustling sackcloth, mumbled prayers – dust. When it was built they must have thought it a permanent monument to God. But it proves to be ephemeral as a whore's love.

Helen What's the matter, husband?

Llewellyn Nothing. The scales fall and the blind man sees. It's all as clear as day.

Helen What is?

Llewellyn The death of love.

Helen Pardon?

Llewellyn I said, *The Death of Love*, the title of my play. Helen . . . you are a whore.

Trevelyn You can't call her that!

Llewellyn Keep out of this, you dog!

Trevelyn How dare you!

Llewellyn You great, lumpen, talentless, deceitful bastard!

Trevelyn Take that back; I am not talentless!

Llewellyn (*drawing his dagger*) This is how I'll take it back.

Trevelyn (*scrambling to his feet*) Ah ha! I see we're leaping forward to the dreary denouement, where the two-dimensional malcontent makes a hackneyed attempt on the life of the hero and is foiled by the hero's vastly superior strength!

Llewellyn Do you want her?

Trevelyn Pardon?

Llewellyn Do you want my wife?

Trevelyn What?

Llewellyn Take her! Let her destroy your peace. Let her be your millstone. I'll have her as mine no longer! (*He turns away.*)

Trevelyn (*pause*) Look, I only kissed her. It was one kiss – scripted by your own hand!

Helen . . . Was there nothing else there?

Trevelyn Helen, there's always something there but it's – well, I get carried away. It's difficult, you know, when you're feeling the moment, not to . . . give it your all, especially when it's a real lady. But I kiss all the time. It's part of my job! . . . It's why I hate the adolescents. They make me feel strange.

Helen (*to herself*) What's to be done? What can I do? . . . My marriage is over. I've kissed an idiot and everything has gone. (*to Llewellyn*) God help me! You don't even see the injustice! You don't see how you have driven me –

Llewellyn Driven you?

Helen *Driven!*

Llewellyn You threw yourself at him!

Helen I was reeling from the shock of someone who kissed me as if I was *real*! To you, I've always been a forbidden delight, a virginal alabaster thing – and now I'm a whore! There's nothing in the middle, is there? No place for a real woman at all! You're a wordsmith; you make words – Tell me, what's he? What is a man-whore?

Trevelyn Pardon?

39

Helen And you, what can I call you that would damage you as much?

Llewellyn Helen.

Helen Drooping, sissy, milksop sap! . . .

Llewellyn Helen!

Helen Impotent bastard prig!

Llewellyn This is demented!

Helen (*calmer*) No. You are an anti-lover.

Llewellyn A what?

Helen An anti-lover, as in the Antichrist. I am married to an anti-lover. Someone who has no conception of love.

Llewellyn I'm an expert on love, Helen; I write about it all the time.

Helen But you don't know how to feel it. I've been married to you for a whole year and all that time I've never felt your love.

Llewellyn Then what is it? Relieve my ignorance and tell me: what is love?

Helen How am I to know, when all I've experienced is disappointment? . . . It's in a face across a table. It's as earthly as eating a meal. It's as common as laughter, and rare as a phoenix egg. It's both transcendent and mundane – and as hard to bind and hold as a moving second of time.

Trevelyn (*to Llewellyn*) Oh that's very good; you should use that.

Llewellyn I thought you formed of the finest stuff. I thought your very breath was made of heaven.

Trevelyn Now, why don't I wait in the cart while you two kiss and make up?

Helen Give me the knife.

Llewellyn (*handing it to her*) Are you contemplating suicide, dear wife?

Helen No. Murder.

> *She stabs him. He gasps. He begins to die. Before Trevelyn can react, she stabs him too. He shrieks, clutching himself. Then both men sheepishly realise they are not wounded. Helen shows them the workings of the theatrical knife.*

Helen It's a pretence. (*to Trevelyn*) Like you. (*to Llewellyn*) And you. (*She stabs herself.*) The death of love.

Scene Five

THE ENLIGHTENMENT

1735. The space has become a town house. Roxanne, a lady, is reading a newspaper. Marianne, a servant, enters.

Roxanne (*without looking up*) Yes?

Marianne The man is here, my lady.

Roxanne lets the newspaper fall to the floor. She takes off her spectacles.

Marianne Would you like me to show him in?

Roxanne He's early. I said not until noon had struck.

Marianne That's what I told him. (*with a slight smirk*) He must be eager, my lady.

Roxanne Are the servants gone?

Marianne Yes, my lady.

Roxanne And my father is asleep?

Marianne Yes, my lady.

Roxanne I want you to sit outside his door. If he so much as stirs, come down *immediately*.

Marianne He won't stir. I gave him the draught with his breakfast. My lady, (shall I fetch the man in . . .)

There is the faintest echo of keening; a sound of anger and rage.

Roxanne Shhh. (*She listens.*) That noise . . .

Marianne I can't hear –

Roxanne There! Listen . . .

The crying fades.

Marianne I'm sorry, I couldn't –

Roxanne It's gone.

Marianne Have you heard it before, my lady?

Roxanne Yes . . . the more I strain my ears, the less I catch of it; it's strange . . . Well. Send him in.

Marianne makes to go. She turns.

Marianne Do you think the place . . . might be haunted, my lady?

Roxanne Ghosts are relics of an age of ignorance, Marianne.

Marianne Only . . . there's a feeling downstairs that . . .

Roxanne That what?

Marianne That it might be.

Roxanne How can it be haunted? It's brand new!

Marianne Yes / but –

Roxanne We're the first family here!

Marianne But sometimes it goes cold / for no reason and –

Roxanne I want to see the man!

Marianne Yes, my lady. (*Marianne goes to pick up the newspaper.*)

Roxanne Leave it. It's for him.

Marianne makes to leave.

Marianne. Thank you for your help in this matter.

Marianne (*with a slight smirk*) It's a pleasure, my lady.

Roxanne If anyone should hear of it, I shall throw you from this house and drag your name through the mud for as long as I draw breath. Do you understand?

Marianne . . . Yes, my lady.

She exits. Roxanne surveys the room.

Roxanne I know what you are . . . And one day I shall find out how to reach you.

Marianne enters.

Marianne The gentleman, my lady.

Marianne shows a Man into the room. He is an artisan, plainly dressed. She leaves. Roxanne locks the door.

Roxanne (*pause*) Good afternoon.

Man Yes, ma'am.

Roxanne Would you stand over there please? On the paper.

The Man walks over to the newspaper. He decides not to stand on it. He looks at Roxanne. She decides not to pursue the matter.

What's your name?

Man Daniel Smith.

Roxanne Do you know who I am, Daniel Smith?

Man I have been told you are a lady who will pay.

Roxanne Have you been told what I want?

Man Yes.

Roxanne Are you prepared to do it?

Man Yes.

Roxanne Then do it.

> *The Man slowly undresses, casting his clothes on the floor. He gets down to his breeches.*

Stop.

> *The Man stops. Roxanne walks around him. She stands in front of him.*

Would you raise your arms above your head, please?

> *The Man does so. Roxanne puts on her spectacles, studies his under-arm hair, then takes them off again.*

I thought so. (*Pause.*) Continue.

> *The Man continues to undress. At last, he is naked. He looks at Roxanne.*

There's no need for you to look at me.

> *The Man slowly averts his eyes.*

God's own image. The mystery, revealed.

> *She giggles. The Man looks at her.*

Do you object to me laughing?

Man You can do what you like.

Roxanne I have never seen a naked man. I'm thirty-three years old, and I've never seen a naked man.

Man The sight is funny then?

> *Roxanne giggles.*

I have never found the sight of a naked woman funny.

Roxanne Don't be offended, please. Laughter doesn't always signify mirth.

The Man looks away. Pause.

I've seen you working across the street. I stand at the window and . . . I see you working, from time to time.

Man I've been here since the building started. I worked on this house too.

Roxanne Did you?

Man There was a ruin here, before.

Roxanne A ruin of what?

Man Dunno. Some kind of a church.

Roxanne A church?

Man Or a prison, something like that. Thick walls; old style. The bricks are part of your foundations.

Roxanne It's strange to think that ten years ago there were fields all around, and now streets, streets and fine houses, as far as you can see. They say there is work here, for generations.

Man Yes.

Roxanne Building a city for the future.

Man Yes.

> *Roxanne puts out a hand to touch him. She removes it. She moves away.*

Roxanne Have you any learning, Daniel?

Man No.

Roxanne I have . . . nothing else but. (*She smiles.*) I am currently acquainting myself with scientific fact, with the mechanical workings of the world, with the mathematics of the spheres, the chemistry of the elements and the dimensions of space. One of the dimensions of space is time. Were you aware of that?

46

Man No, lady.

Roxanne It is the element of change. Do you ever wish you could change time?

Man I do not know.

Roxanne You never feel that time is an ungovernable tyranny over which we have no control?

Man I'm not sure.

Roxanne It ploughs onwards in an invincible line from past to future and our whole lives, from mewling to infirmity, are mere breaths upon its way. I'd say that was tyrannous. Would you not agree?

Man I have never thought about it.

Roxanne But if you were to think about it, what would you think? Would you come to question time, as I have, to question the justice of its nature? Would you perhaps come to think, as I do, that in a world of such change, time cannot be unchangeable?

Man I do not know.

Roxanne Supposing that time was not a line, but a sphere in which we could envisage a flow in both directions? Supposing it were possible to empirically investigate the structure of time and . . . and to change it?

Man To change time?

Roxanne Yes. We perceive time as a series of apparently indivisible moments, but supposing one could divide each moment and move between them? One would find oneself in a plenitude of ages, different worlds of endless possibility, a landscape of time that was nebulous and not definite, so that one was not confined to a particular age or sphere or set of circumstances so that . . . that one, in a way, could be free?

Man (*pause*) God makes us free, lady.

Roxanne is suddenly embarrassed.

The next world is timeless, they say.

Roxanne I'm sorry . . .

Man A heavenly paradise without time. Is that what you mean?

Roxanne Yes . . . (*She smiles, hurt.*) That's it exactly.

Pause.

Are you cold?

Man Not very.

Roxanne You're very clean.

Man I washed.

Roxanne I didn't ask you here to listen to me speak . . .

Man No.

Roxanne Would you turn your back to me?

The Man turns his back. Roxanne slowly approaches him.

I wish . . . to touch you.

Man All right.

Roxanne touches the Man's back. She closes her eyes and turns her face away. Her hand moves over his skin, eventually coming to rest. She removes it.

Roxanne I want to do something.

Man You may do what you like.

Roxanne embraces the back of the Man. She holds him closely, resting her head on him. It moves her. She is crying, silently. At last, she releases him. She stands apart, trying to compose herself. The Man turns round. He sees the consternation on Roxanne's face. She still has her eyes shut. He gently tries to kiss her.

Roxanne (*recoiling in shock*) Who told you to do that?

Man You are upset –

Roxanne Who said you could?

Man No one.

Roxanne Turn your back!

The Man turns from Roxanne. Roxanne recovers herself.

Dress.

Man Lady –

Roxanne I said dress. I've seen enough.

Man (*beginning to dress*) Forgive me. I thought / you wanted –

Roxanne It's not your place to think; you have no learning.

Man I thought you wanted love.

Roxanne Love? (*laughing*) *Love?* Is this what you call love?

Man Then what?

Roxanne To empirically investigate the nature of man.

Man And have you?

Roxanne Dress.

Man (*pause*) Are you afraid, lady? Is that why you cry?

Roxanne I said *dress*!

The Man continues to dress. He approaches Roxanne.

Man You think us different. But if you were naked too, we would be the same.

Roxanne We would not.

Man Our clothes make us different, that's all. But in the simple way of things we are the same.

Roxanne There is no simple way of things! If there was a simple way of anything, do you think I'd be here? With you? And how can we ever, ever be the same?

Man We are the same before God.

Roxanne God is not present here! God has not been witness to anything that's passed between us.

Man Nothing has passed between us, lady.

Roxanne throws a purse of money. It lands at the Man's feet.

Roxanne It has now.

Scene Six

THE ROMANTIC AGE

1823. The attic of the town house. Miss Tilly, a governess, and Mr Quilley, her employer, are having sexual intercourse.

Miss Tilly And so he struggles as hard as he can against the effects of the drug, but it has rendered him dumb and too weak to fight. Then the governess, with almost preternatural strength, drags him upstairs to the attic, where she proceeds to tie him in chains.

Mr Quilley Yes –

Miss Tilly She leaves him lying on a bed of straw with a bowl of rank water, cruelly placed too far away for him to reach.

Mr Quilley Oh –

Miss Tilly Too late has he come to see that there is evil in her heart –

Mr Quilley Oh yes –

Miss Tilly – evil that will wreak havoc with all that he holds dear. That night, when he finally recovers the strength to cry out –

Mr Quilley Yes –

Miss Tilly – the governess springs up the stairs, her tresses loose, her poplin nightgown –

Mr Quilley Uh –

Miss Tilly – shimmering in candlelight. She approaches and slaps him –

Mr Quilley Oh –

Miss Tilly –and stuffs a gag in his mouth.

Mr Quilley Ah –

Miss Tilly She kicks him brutally –

Mr Quilley AH!

Miss Tilly – and burns his facial hair with her candle.

Mr Quilley reaches a climax.

'You fool,' says the governess with an icy smile, 'I've told your wife you're dead, consumed by a disease so contagious that even to view your corpse would render her in danger. She leaves for Derbyshire at dawn, never to return, for I have bribed the coachman to see that calamity befalls her.'

Mr Quilley Miss Tilley . . .

Miss Tilly 'I am to stay here alone, chief beneficiary of your last will and testament.'

Mr Quilley I am done . . .

Miss Tilly 'You shall be locked in this attic for ever, fed on dog scraps, chained and beaten like a beast until slowly, the terror and the isolation send you howling mad.' And then she laughs. Like this. (*She laughs.*)

Mr Quilley (*extricating himself*) Well, that's a jolly good story . . .

Miss Tilly Yes. It's one of several that I'm working on. There's a tremendous market for them.

Mr Quilley I'm sure.

Miss Tilly I was wondering, Mr Quilley, could you find me a publisher?

Millie enters, heavily pregnant. Mr Quilley and Miss Tilly spring apart.

Millie Oh, here you are . . .

Mr Quilley Darling, you shouldn't come up the stairs. It's far too dangerous!

Millie I missed you . . . And I half wondered if we had a ghost. I thought I heard strange laughing.

Mr Quilley Ah, that was Miss Tilly.

Miss Tilly Mr Quilley was telling me a very amusing story.

Mr Quilley Yes . . . I was helping Miss Tilley to put away some old toys and I was relating to her how little Billy ruined my jacket by vomiting all over it, just as I was due to give my first speech in the House.

Millie Oh yes, poor fellow . . . He had colic. (*Pause.*) The children are asking for you, Miss Tilly.

Miss Tilly (*making to leave*) Thank you for helping me with the toys, sir.

Miss Tilly exits.

Mr Quilley I'm very cross with you for coming up here. What if you'd fallen?

Millie Oh my love, you'd always be there to catch me, if I fell. (*She embraces him.*)

Mr Quilley Millie . . .

Millie Do you know, I was sitting downstairs thinking of every way in which my life is blessed and I was suddenly overcome with a feeling so strong that I had to find you and share it. It's happiness, my darling. I'm so happy . . .

Mr Quilley Millie, you sweet thing . . .

Millie Here I am in my beautiful home, with the best of all men. I'm so, so happy . . . it makes me want to cry.

Mr Quilley holds her closer. They continue to embrace while De Vere enters and the space becomes . . .

Scene Seven

THE AGE OF EMPIRE

1898. A shabby, bohemian studio. De Vere, a gentleman, is gazing at an unpainted canvas, which stands on an easel. Evening.

De Vere (*examining the easel*) Yes . . . Like a darkness, shining in the light.

There is a knock at his door. He answers it.
Buttermere, a vicar, is on the threshold.

Buttermere! . . . I was beginning to give up hope.

Buttermere I've had the most awful trouble finding you.

De Vere Not a part of town one often comes, I know.

Buttermere I wasn't sure I'd got the right address. It's awfully rough out there, De Vere. All sorts of unrepeatable things said to me as I passed.

De Vere Consign them to oblivion, my friend, and have a drink.

Buttermere I think I need one. I have just heard the word for a man's organ come from the mouth of a woman.

De Vere (*amused*) Goodness . . . (*Hands Buttermere a drink.*) Well, here's to you. Your good health.

Buttermere And yours. It's wonderful to see you again.

De Vere Yes.

Buttermere After all this time.

De Vere Wonderful.

Buttermere You haven't changed at all, you know.

De Vere Oh, I have. Deeply. Nothing changes a man like travel.

Buttermere Well –

De Vere I've seen dawn over a thousand different horizons, from Cairo to the Southern Cape. How can one eat lotus by the banks of the Nile and not return a different man?

Buttermere I don't know . . . (*Pause.*) Well, interesting sort of place you've got.

De Vere My studio. It's in a dreadful state; the roof leaks, the area's a slum, but I like it. Sometimes I work here until late and the idea of going home is more than I can bear. So I have everything I need, right here. This is my empire, Buttermere, and in it I lay out the canvas of humanity.

Buttermere Gosh.

De Vere I returned home when I discovered that a man with an easel needs only his imagination to travel. He can be both hermit and explorer in one small room.

Buttermere Well yes . . .

De Vere Days have gone by when I have been so lost in the forgetfulness of the creative mind that the outside world ceases to have any meaning and I exist only in the reality of art.

Buttermere I can't tell you how thrilled I was to hear you'd become a painter. I knew you'd do something brilliant with your life. Even at school you were . . . well, you shone. I always thought so, anyway. I was hoping you'd show me some of your work.

De Vere I'd love to. But the light's terrible. At this late hour you wouldn't get a proper impression.

Buttermere I'm sure I would.

De Vere Besides, I fear you might find my art a little shocking.

Buttermere Why?

De Vere I paint ladies of the night.

Buttermere Oh! . . . I thought you painted scenes from antiquity.

De Vere I do. But my sitters are ladies of the night.

Buttermere Well, I – Gracious . . . What are they like?

De Vere Much the same as ladies of the day. Only they don't mind sharing their secrets. In fact, for a coin or two, they'll share anything. (*He smiles.*) I'd forgotten that expression. Do you know, sometimes I used to bait you, just so you'd gaze at me like that.

   Buttermere lowers his gaze.

I knew you'd join the church.

Buttermere I almost didn't.

De Vere I knew you would.

Buttermere Well. It seemed . . . the best thing. And frankly, I don't know what else I would have done. I was never bright, like you.

De Vere Was it the right choice? Are you happy?

Buttermere Oh yes. Of course I am. Why are you looking at me in that way?

De Vere In what way?

Buttermere In that infernal way. As if you want me to tell you I'm miserable.

De Vere Are you miserable?

Buttermere No. I have a thriving parish and a lovely wife . . .

De Vere You're married?

Buttermere Yes, yes, of course. Aren't you?

De Vere No.

Buttermere Oh, you ought to marry, you know.

De Vere Why?

Buttermere Well . . . it's what a man does. A wife makes a man complete.

De Vere Am I incomplete?

Buttermere No, but De Vere, if you were to, to meet the right girl and settle down, then . . . I suppose what I'm thinking is . . . that our wives could be friends.

De Vere You want me to marry so that our wives could be friends?

Buttermere Lavinia could do with a friend – I mean a friend like you've always been to me.

De Vere Are you not Lavinia's friend?

Buttermere Well, yes, but she doesn't talk to me, you know? In fact, she rarely talks at all. She has the curtains closed most of the time and she just –

De Vere Just what?

Buttermere Oh, you don't want to hear all this.

De Vere Of course I do. You used to tell me everything.

Buttermere Well, Lavinia is just a little quiet, that's all.

De Vere A little quiet?

Buttermere But she takes tincture of opium for her health and they say it can be quite a dampener on the spirits. She's very sensitive.

De Vere Poor Lavinia.

Buttermere And she's –

De Vere She's what?

Buttermere (*pause. Sighing*) I haven't seen you for the best part of ten years. I'm with you less than five minutes and I find myself telling you things I wouldn't tell anyone.

De Vere You haven't told me anything. My friend . . . Why don't we have another drink?

Buttermere I shouldn't have had that one.

De Vere Let me fill your glass. (*De Vere takes Buttermere's glass and fills it.*) This is the water of Lethe, which flows like a ribbon of light through the land of the dark. Those who drink it shall forget all pain and be reborn. Such is the power of liquor; it makes innocents of us all. (*handing Buttermere his glass*) To our friendship.

Buttermere Yes. To us.

They drink a toast.

De Vere There is a reason I asked you to meet me here and not at the club. It's your face.

Buttermere My face?

De Vere I've got into the habit of searching people's faces. It's what one does as an artist. When I ran into you, after all this time, your face – the light you had in your eyes, the openness of your expression – it inspired me. I want to paint you.

Buttermere To *paint* me?

De Vere I'd be honoured if you'd let me.

Buttermere (*bashfully*) Well . . . I'm profoundly moved. You really think I'm worth a portrait?

De Vere I most certainly do. You have singular qualities, my friend.

Buttermere I wouldn't have thought vicars were a very inspiring subject.

De Vere I don't wish to paint you as a vicar.

Buttermere Oh?

De Vere This isn't an ordinary portrait. I don't wish to paint you as you, at all.

Buttermere Am I to be a figure from antiquity?

De Vere In a way. Don't get me wrong here, old friend. I want to paint you as Satan.

Buttermere *What?*

De Vere Or should I say Lucifer. Lucifer, before he fell.

Buttermere That's not funny, De Vere.

De Vere I don't intend it to be. When I saw you, an image leapt into my mind, so suddenly. I thought, 'The Son of the Morning, First Archangel of the Heavenly Host, Lucifer, Prince of this World!' I saw you like a dazzling darkness shining in the light. (*Pause.*) Does the idea appeal?

Buttermere Look at me. How is it possible that I make you think of Lucifer?

De Vere Before he fell. My dear fellow, you're as beautiful as an angel.

Buttermere Don't be ridiculous –

De Vere And there's something in you, stirring in the heart of you, that wishes to rebel, to throw in God and all of his works –

Buttermere What!?

De Vere Something that desires freedom. I can see it in your face.

Buttermere Nonsense.

De Vere Put down your drink.

Buttermere Why should I?

De Vere I want you to take your clothes off.

Buttermere What for!?

De Vere I want you in a pose of innocence, as if receiving benediction from your maker.

Buttermere Absolutely not!

De Vere And at the moment of blessing, you realise a basic truth: your maker didn't make you at all. You are as fundamental a part of the universe as he is. You are the father of desire and one cannot have life without desire.

Buttermere You can't ask me to blaspheme!

De Vere I want to capture the moment when you realise the nature of the thing that you are; when you understand your potential. I want to paint your first free thought. It's not blasphemous, it's profound. (*Pause.*) The title is 'The Birth Of Love'.

Buttermere The birth of evil –

De Vere The birth of love – because love is nobler than worship, love cannot be kept in ignorant submission;

love is only holy when it's free. Real love requires knowledge and free will. Lucifer gave us both. And if those things represent evil to you then I really don't know what to say.

Buttermere (*pause*) You know, if anyone looks like Satan here, it's you.

De Vere (*smiling wryly*) I'm sure my life is in my face, just as yours is. If you let me paint you, I shall tell you. Let me paint you and I shall tell you my whole journey down the primrose path. Then afterwards, if you wish to, you can save my soul.

Buttermere (*pause*) Get me another drink . . .

De Vere We shall paint the truth. It will be you and I together!

Buttermere Get me a drink!

> *De Vere pours Buttermere a drink. He downs it in one. He takes off his jacket.*

You could always make me do anything for you.

De Vere I have never made you do anything that you didn't want to do.

> *Buttermere begins to take his collar off. De Vere helps. He throws it on the floor.*

Buttermere My shackles. That's what you think, isn't it? You think I'm in shackles.

> *De Vere slides his arms around Buttermere and holds him, with compassion.*

I hate my life, De Vere. What am I to do?

De Vere I don't know.

> *They are still.*

*Buttermere turns and embraces De Vere. They hold
each other tightly. They kiss.*

*Buttermere walks to a position by the canvas. He
takes off his shirt.*

Buttermere You wish to capture . . . (*He lets the shirt
fall to the ground.*) . . . my first free thought.

Scene Eight

THE AGE OF AUSTERITY

1932. A dingy bedsit. A Boy is standing in shabby underwear. Joy, a prostitute, lies barely clad on a bed. The Boy looks devastated. He picks up his shirt from the floor – the position where Buttermere dropped his. He begins to dress. Joy watches. As the Boy does up his shirt, he goes to the window. He looks out. Pause.

Joy What's it like out there?

Boy Fog.

Joy Still foggy is it?

Boy Yes.

Joy Everything disappears when it's like that. Just this room and nothing else.

> *The Boy looks at her, disturbed by what she has said. He continues to dress. Joy lights herself a cigarette. She holds it up.*

D'you want one o' these?

Boy No thank you.

Joy You know you got another ten minutes yet. (*Pause.*) You don't have to go for another ten minutes. You paid for half an hour. So you don't have to go yet.

Boy (*doing up his school tie*) I have to.

Joy You gonna find your way in all that fog?

Boy Yes.

Joy (*pause*) This your first time?

Boy No.

Joy D'you mind me asking?

Boy No.

Joy You don't have to go. You got another ten minutes. You can try again if you like. There's no shame in it.

Boy (*rapidly pulling on a school blazer*) No.

Joy Might make you feel better.

Boy No!

Joy Was it me? . . .

The Boy goes to the door. He tries it. It appears to be locked. He pulls and pulls it, in a rapidly growing panic. He becomes frantic. He is almost at the point of shrieking when he stops and attempts to control himself.

I put the bolt in. Up at the top. Sometimes the other girls walk in.

The Boy looks up. He draws back the bolt. He looks at the door. He bursts into tears. He sobs, with his head against the door. Joy puts out her cigarette. She sits. She despairs.

Flynn enters. She takes the blankets off Joy's bed and wraps them round her, as the space becomes . . .

Scene Nine

THE AGE OF INNOCENCE

1969. A squat. Flynn starts to take her clothes off under the blankets. She is shivering, trying to keep herself warm. The room has a screen with badly painted murals across it.

Flynn Any progress in there?

Quinn (*behind the screen*) No.

Flynn How long's it gonna take? . . . 'Cause we said turn up from ten.

Quinn I can't get the connection! The electric's about a million years old.

Flynn Well, maybe we should just put some money in the meter.

Quinn (*appearing*) This is about free love, isn't it?

Flynn (*starting to stuff her clothes into a binbag*) Yes.

Quinn So if it's free, why should we put money in the meter?

Flynn 'Cause it's freezing. No one's gonna even take their jumpers off if it's like this – never mind getting naked.

Quinn Have you got any money?

Flynn No.

Quinn Well, I haven't either.

Flynn Oh.

Quinn So let's do it my way, OK? (*Flynn nods.*) Give us a peek.

Flynn briefly opens her blankets.

Take your socks off.

Flynn I'm too cold.

Quinn Sissy. (*Quinn goes behind the screens.*)

Flynn Quinn?

Quinn Yeh?

Flynn Are you really going to, you know, like go all the way?

Quinn Well, that's sort of the point, isn't it?

Flynn Yeh, I know, only –

Quinn What?

Flynn Now we've come to it . . .

Quinn What? (*appearing again, irritated*) What?

Flynn I'm a bit nervous. That's all.

Quinn Why are you nervous?

Flynn Well, I know we'll all be blindfold and everything –

Quinn Yeh –

Flynn – which is a great idea, really innovative – so it's all about touch and feeling rather than the aesthetic, yeh, but suppose your blindfold slips right, and you find yourself doing it with someone you know, like fat or repulsive –

Quinn It's not about that, is it?

Flynn Yeh I know, but supposing it's like a dirty old man or something.

Quinn We haven't invited any dirty old men! Jesus, Flynn, you're very good at lapping up all the theory, being all keen and eager, but then, when it actually comes to the point of action, you're like a little nun.

Flynn Don't say that.

Quinn This is important for us. It's about the emancipation of love. People we dig, coming together to share the miracle of sex, turning all that amazing energy into a positive force for change, a force for peace. It's about revolutionising the whole way we are with one another, creating something completely new for the future.

Flynn I know –

Quinn Getting rid of the ownership, the possession, the jealousy. It's about freedom, freedom of love. And a lot of people have lost their lives for that.

Flynn But we have freedom of love, don't we? I mean, just you and me?

Quinn We have a beautiful thing. That's why we have to share it with others, baby. It's selfish to keep it to ourselves. I don't wanna possess you. It's bourgeois.

Flynn So we have to be generous even to spotty, pongy, bad-breath people?

Quinn Look, if my blindfold slips, and I find I'm doing it with some less than dazzling chick, I'm not gonna stop, am I? She'd be hurt. (*Pause.*) I'm going in the loft. (*He disappears behind the screen. As he exits:*) It's weird, this place. There's stuff up there that gives me the creeps; freaky paintings and pigeon bones.

Lynne and Gwyn enter. Flynn rushes behind the screen and turns away from them.

Lynne Is this it?

Gwyn It can't be . . .

Flynn Hello. Hi!

68

Gwyn Is this the Love-In?

Lynne We found your invite yeh? Thought it would be a bit more happening . . .

Flynn Yeh but . . . We're not ready yet, OK?

Lynne Oh.

Flynn Um, you're a bit early. 'Cause we're trying to tap into the mains yeh, so that the corporate pigs can pay for it, but Quinn, that's my boyfriend – like in a non-ownership way? – hasn't actually got it together. He can't get a connection.

Gwyn Why are you hiding?

Flynn 'Cause I um – look, there's some binliners out there, yeh? And some labels? And some blindfolds, so take your clothes off, put them in a binbag, stick a label on it with your name on, yeh, and then put a blindfold on and come behind here and this is where it's all gonna be happening. Only it's a bit cold 'til we get the heating on.

Gwyn Are we the first here?

Flynn Um, yeh, but don't let that bother you.

Lynne 'Cause we don't wanna end up just doing it with each other.

Gwyn We do that all the time.

Lynne And we're sick of it. Actually.

Gwyn That's why we've come.

Lynne I mean we love each other, yeh, but the spark's gone.

Flynn Right –

Gwyn You know, it always does. You always end up thinking this is really mundane, man.

Lynne So we're still a couple but we need Dr Illicit Sex to keep us, you know . . .

Gwyn Hot.

Flynn Well, d'you wanna come back later when it's all like a bit warmer even?

Gwyn Not really, no.

Flynn Or you could start with Quinn, I s'pose.

Lynne What, both of us?

Flynn He's definitely up for it. Shall I shout him?

Gwyn I don't wanna shag another bloke.

Lynne He's sick of that as well. He's sick of everything.

Gwyn No I'm not.

Lynne Yes you are; you've glutted yourself on pornography.

Gwyn So?

Lynne It's boring.

Gwyn (*to Flynn*) What about you, babe? Why don't you and me start it?

Flynn Um . . .

Gwyn You got three tits or something? That why you're hiding?

Flynn We're not supposed to see each other, 'cause we're all blindfold, so the intensity of touch is like, much more?

Lynne Oh great. It'll be a relief not to have to see anyone's face. 'Specially his.

Gwyn Let's start then, babe. And your boyfriend can join in.

Flynn Um, I can't. Sorry.

Lynne Why not?

Flynn Well actually, I got my period. So I'm just sort of here doing the snacks and drinks and that.

Gwyn I don't care about your period.

Lynne Neither do I, sister.

Flynn Yeh . . . but I got a rash. As well. So I can't. Well I could, but . . . I wouldn't if I were you. You'd be better off waiting for someone else.

Gwyn Jesus.

Lynne She's a scared kid . . .

Gwyn Oh for fuck's sake. I thought this was adults only.

Lynne Come on. We can pick someone up in the pub more easily than this.

Gwyn Why don't we just go home? I'll make myself pretend you're someone else.

Lynne Yeh well. You can pretend I'm someone who's bloody well asleep. 'Cause I will be.

Gwyn What a waste o' time.

They leave. Flynn reappears. She ties her blindfold on. She is close to tears.

Flynn I *will* do it. I *can* do it. I will emancipate love. I have to liberate myself. Freedom of love . . . freedom of love . . .

The electricity comes on; psychedelic lights, loud music. Quinn whoops.

Quinn (*off*) Let's rock!

Flynn whimpers. She pulls the blankets over her head.

Scene Ten

THE AGE OF EXCESS

The present. The space has become a brand new office building: a dating agency. A video plays. We see a logo for 'Hearts International, the exclusive place to find love' and then an image of Brigitta.

Brigitta Um, hello, my name's Brigitta . . . and I've never done anything like this. Um, I'm thirty (-three), I'm single and . . . I mean a lot of you will probably be fast-forwarding already but for those of you who are still here . . . I'm a really decent person and you'd be lucky to get me, so if you're a *proper* man . . . (*She sighs.*) . . . why on earth would you be looking at this? (*a moment of static*) Hi, I'm Brigitta. I'm thirty, I'm single and I'm looking for . . . (*She puts her head in hands.*) Anything –

> *Rita enters. She picks up a remote control and watches, her feet on Anita's desk.*

Anything . . . (*brightly*) So if you're shallow and sleazy and you'd like a meaningless, depressing encounter, why don't you – (*static*) Hi, I'm Brigitta. (*Pause.*) I can't do this.

> *Rita fast-forwards.*

It's like there's this chasm – Oh, I don't know. I feel as if I'm standing on some kind of an ice floe and the rest of humanity is just drifting further and further away. I feel *so alone* . . . And it's not just me; all of us. We're – we don't have enough – I don't know – whatever it is . . . whatever it is that makes swans stay together.

Rita Oh my God.

Brigitta They never part. Once they meet, that's it, for life. Would you say that was love or just some kind of instinct? Blackbirds do it too.

Rita Fuck's sake.

Brigitta Sorry. I'm really sorry. (*Static. Much more brightly*) Hi, I'm Brigitta. I'm twenty-nine, I'm a Gemini, I like music, travel, dining out and life's simple pleasures. So, if you're aged between thirty and forty, if you're looking for friendship, fun and a bit of sunshine in your life, why don't you give me a call?

Rita (*spelling it out*) S-a-d-d-o.

Anita enters, hurried. Rita flicks the video off.

Anita Hi, sorry, some ball-less little no-dick tried to clamp me. I had to spend twenty minutes trying to convince him that I was thick and he was gorgeous before he'd let me go – cunt. Any messages?

Rita Don't you think you should knock before you come in?

Anita Rita, / are there any –

Rita I don't like your tone. You should address me as Miss Clark. And knock before you come in. I could have been doing anything in here.

Anita (*amused*) Really?

Rita Anything.

Anita Sorry, Miss Clark, but the saddos are going to be here in about five minutes. I need to check everything's ready.

Rita Everything's fine. Take your jacket off.

Anita Rita –

Rita Miss Clark. Get it off.

  Anita undoes her jacket.

Throw it on the floor.

  Anita is tempted.

Anita I haven't got time . . .

Rita Unbutton your shirt and come here.

Anita Baby . . . I haven't got / time.

Rita I'm not your baby.

  Pause.

Anita Sorry.

Rita You never have time.

Anita Can't we do something later? After the saddos.

Rita I'm busy later.

Anita Doing what?

  Rita says nothing. She removes her feet from the desk.

God . . . I've only just walked in the door and already
I'm in the doghouse.

Rita You don't give a shit about me, do you?

Anita Oh come on.

Rita Say it then.

Anita Say what?

Rita Say it.

Anita (*pause*) I won't be forced. (*She starts checking that
everything is ready.*)

Rita You know it amazes me that someone who spends her whole life shoving romance down people's throats is so terrified of the whole idea of love that she can't even bring herself to say the word.

Anita Rita, if you're going to be a pain in the arse, can you just go home?

Rita Oh, I wouldn't dream of it. Let me give you your messages and while I'm at it why don't I suck your cock?

Anita You are so childish.

Rita (*leafing through a notepad*) The photocopier bloke can't get here until Monday. *Home and Garden* are doing a deal on advertising space, half a page for the price of a quarter. And sticky-out-chin-woman isn't coming.

Anita What?

Rita Yep. She's found love on a chat-page.

Anita She *what*?

Rita I told her she'd never get our kind of exclusive clientele on a website but she said she didn't care. She's been communicating with some bloke from Ramsgate who understands her pain.

Anita You're joking!

Rita I said have you sent him a photo yet? But she didn't deign to reply.

Anita You told me everything was ready!

Rita It is. I put the nibbles out; the champagne's in a bucket.

Anita Have you tried to get someone else?

Rita At an hour's notice?

Anita Well, what are we going to do?

Rita (*unconcerned*) I don't know.

Anita I've got two blokes and only one woman!

Rita Lucky old her.

Anita This is the kind of thing that brings down my name! They're all new – new clients, and I've set them up in a fucking threesome.

Rita They might enjoy it.

There is the faintest echo of keening, a sound of anger and rage.

Anita I needed sticky-out-chin-woman for weird-doctor. She's the only one I could rely on to make him / feel he wasn't (the ugliest person in the room) –

Rita Shhh!

Anita What?

Rita That noise.

Anita What noise?

Rita There.

Anita I can't hear anything.

Rita Shhh!

The crying stops.

Anita . . . I think this place is haunted.

Anita Don't be stupid. It's brand new; we're the first people to lease it.

Rita I know it's new, but it's built on top of old stuff.

Anita Of course it is. We're right in the middle of the city.

Rita Yes, but there might be an Inca burial ground underneath or something. Or a pet cemetery; something unrestful. I'm not being funny. The place goes cold sometimes.

Anita You think my office is haunted by a dead pet?

Rita You know what I mean!

Anita Frankly, Rita, I'm more concerned with what to do when the saddos get here.

Rita It's probably my juvenile dementia, that's what you're thinking, isn't it?

Anita (*coldly*) I don't think you can ever assume to know what I'm thinking.

Rita Do you know what I'm thinking?

Anita No.

Rita (*icily*) Good.

There's a buzz on the intercom.

Anita Shit.

Rita I'm going home, OK?

Anita Don't!

Rita I've got to pluck my toenails.

Anita Don't. Please Reet, you can't. (*into the intercom*) Hello? (*to Rita*) Wait! (*into the intercom*) Hi, Dieter! (*She buzzes him in. To Rita*) I'm sorry. I've been an absolute cow since the moment I got in and I'm really sorry. I'll make it up to you any way I can – but right now you have to be the other woman.

Rita What?

Anita Pretend to be the other saddo. Please. I'd do it myself, only they've all met me.

Rita Are you serious?

Anita You don't have to go on a date with them or anything. You just have to meet them for half an hour, make an excuse and leave.

Rita I don't believe it.

Anita Please, *please*, Rita; I'll meet you later, we'll go out, I'll buy you dinner –

Rita You PIMP!

Dieter enters.

Dieter Hello.

Anita Dieter, so glad you could make it.

Dieter Am I the first?

Anita No, this is . . . Lolita.

Rita looks at her aghast.

She's a new client too.

Dieter Hello.

Rita Hi.

Dieter holds out his hand. Rita shakes it.

Anita So, would you guys like a glass of champagne?

Dieter I'll just have a mineral water, thanks.

Rita I'll have champagne. Lots of it.

Anita Cool. Back in two nanoseconds. (*She exits.*)

Rita So you don't drink?

Dieter No.

Rita Are you pregnant or something?

Dieter Er no . . . I'm a recovering alcoholic.

Rita Oh. How long have you been sober?

Dieter Two years.

Rita What made you give up?

Dieter The realisation of what had made me drink.

Rita What had made you drink?

Dieter Terror.

Rita Terror?

Dieter Yes, I think so. (*attempting to change the subject*) So how / about you?

Rita What made you realise that? Only I'm thinking of becoming an alcoholic myself and I thought maybe you could tell me if it was worthwhile.

Dieter I can't be glib about it, I'm sorry.

Rita No, I'm sorry . . . I'm really glib and sorry.

Dieter That's OK.

Rita What were you terrified of?

Dieter Well . . . if you want the whole story, I was reaching for the Scotch one night –

Anita enters, with a bottle of champagne.

Anita Just opening this; I haven't gone away!

Rita We're fine.

Dieter And I was suddenly convulsed with pain and I looked down and a blotch had appeared on my skin, a huge, dark, mottled bruise, right over my liver . . .

Rita Oh / my God!

The buzzer goes. Anita goes to answer it.

Dieter And of course I blacked out as usual and remembered nothing, but in the morning when I woke up, the bruise was still there and I couldn't move with the pain.

Anita (*into the buzzer*) Hi, sweetheart, come on up!

Dieter So. I lay in bed and thought long and hard about dying.

Anita Yep – Oh!

Dieter I thought this is what I've been trying to do for years, this must be what I want.

Anita Cool, great! (*She exits.*)

Dieter And then at some point in the afternoon I had a kind of a well, I suppose a – I've never really known how to describe it. It was like an incredible sense of calm . . . and I realised that I was no longer afraid. Because what had always terrified me more than death . . . was life. I was terrified of life. And I thought that if I chose, I could stop being afraid. I could decide to live. So, two years later, here I am . . . trying to live.

Rita is moved. Anita returns, followed by Brigitta and Peter.

Anita Now that's what I call handy, meeting on the stairs! Who'd like a glass / of bubbly?

Brigitta Please.

Peter Thanks.

Dieter / So anyway, now I'm terribly embarrassed, so –

Rita Don't be. I think you're very brave. And honest.

Anita pops the bottle.

Anita That's the sound I like to hear!

Rita You make me feel ashamed.

Dieter What of?

Brigitta (*looking nervously at the furnishings*) This is nice . . .

Rita My name isn't Lolita.

Dieter Oh?

Rita It's Rita Clark. My last relationship was with a woman.

Peter (*to Brigitta*) Very soft . . .

Rita I'm confused, you see.

Dieter Well, a lot of us are.

Anita (*handing the glasses round*) Brigitta.

Brigitta Thanks.

Anita Peter.

Peter Jolly good.

Rita I shouldn't be here.

Anita (*handing her a drink*) Of course you should! And an aqua-fizzy for Dieter.

Dieter Thanks.

Anita Here we go. Cheers folks. Welcome to Hearts International.

    They awkwardly clink glasses.

Now, I call evenings like this 'Icebreakers' and they're all about you breaking the ice with one another, having a friendly, open chat with no strings attached, before embarking on the hazardous business of choosing a date.

I never invite more than four specially selected clients, so you don't feel crowded out and you can all get an idea of the kind of exclusive people we have on our books. So, I'm going to take a back seat, sort out the canapés, and leave you to say hello. OK? (*Anita moves to one side. She keeps one ear on Dieter and Rita.*)

Peter It sounds like organs for transplant, doesn't it?

Brigitta Pardon?

Peter Hearts International.

Brigitta Oh. Right . . .

Peter You know, one of those dodgy agencies that buy bodily organs from the poor and disadvantaged.

Rita (*to Dieter*) This woman I was seeing . . .

Brigitta Mmm.

Peter Kidneys and the odd lung / and what-have-you.

Rita / I've decided. I'm gonna dump her completely.

Dieter Oh?

Rita 'Cause sometimes I just think she's out to twist me up inside. She thinks I act like a kid but actually, / she's the childish one.

Peter / I'm a doctor.

Brigitta That's / nice.

Dieter / Oh dear.

Rita You know, she plays manipulative games.

Brigitta Do you specialise in anything?

Rita Sometimes she'll dump me in awkward situations –

Peter Yes I do.

Rita Just to watch me sink or swim –

Peter I'm a urologist.

Brigitta Oh.

Peter That's waterworks / .

Brigitta Yes, I know.

Rita / She holds back affection to punish me for her own stupid past –

Peter Well, not waterworks actually –

Rita And she's never ever, not even once, said she loves me.

Peter That's just a stupid / expression I use –

Rita Do you know what that's like?

Dieter I can imagine.

Peter Because for some reason people seem to be embarrassed / talking about their urinary tracts.

Rita / It's why I want to change.

Brigitta I'm not.

Rita I'm gonna kick her out of my life.

Peter Yes, you see? Where would we be without them? Certainly not drinking champagne! (*He is laughing.*)

Rita I want to know what it's like being with a man.

Peter We'd all be carrying catheters about, wouldn't we?

Rita A good, nice man.

Dieter Oh, right. Well, good luck . . .

Anita (*relieved at Dieter's reply*) Is anybody ready for a top-up? Lolita?

Rita holds out her glass. Anita tops it up.

Goodness, aren't you thirsty.

Peter (*moving across*) Is your name Lolita?

Rita No.

Peter Our hostess just called you Lolita.

Rita It's a *nom de plume*.

Brigitta (*to Anita*) Could I trouble you? . . .

Anita No problem, sweetheart. (*Anita pours Brigitta some champagne.*)

Peter Are you a writer?

Rita No.

Peter Then why have you got a *nom de plume*?

Rita I don't know. Why do you care?

Peter Well, my cat's called Lolita.

Anita No! . . . (*She laughs uproariously.*)

Peter I've got two cats and a terrapin.

Anita Great. (*She exits.*)

Brigitta (*shyly, to Dieter*) Hi, I'm Brigitta.

Dieter Hi. Dieter.

Brigitta Have you been to one of these things before?

Dieter No.

Brigitta Me neither.

Dieter Oh.

Brigitta It's very . . .

Dieter and Brigitta are tongue-tied. The attraction between them is obvious.

Peter My cats are called Lolita and Lucretzia and the terrapin's a male. He's called Severin.

Rita Severin the terrapin?

Peter Yes.

Rita I hate cats.

Brigitta I'm . . . I'm divorced. With two kids.

Peter So, if your name's not Lolita, what is it?

Rita Rita Clark.

Peter Why did you lie?

Rita I didn't.

Peter You obviously did.

Rita A *nom de plume* isn't a lie, it's a *nom de plume*.

Dieter I'm a recovering alcoholic.

Brigitta Oh . . .

Peter It's a false name, a falsehood. Why did you come here with a false name?

Rita I didn't. Who are you anyway, the Spanish Inquisition?

Peter No, I'm just an ordinary, fee-paying client and I got given strict instructions not to lie on my form.

Brigitta . . . Would you like to go?

Rita I don't remember that instruction.

Dieter What, just leave?

Rita Perhaps I ignored it.

Brigitta Yes . . .

Peter So you admit to lying?

Dieter You want to leave . . . with me?

Brigitta nods.

Rita As a matter of fact, my entire form is a web of deceit.

Anita (*entering with canapés*) Now then, who'd like a nibble? Peter?

Peter helps himself. Dieter and Brigitta are gazing at one another.

Peter So, what did you lie about?

Rita I said my favourite colour was blue when really it's green. I said I was a lapdancer when really I'm a temp.

Peter I don't believe you.

Rita I said I could breathe underwater when really I can't. And that sometimes I get stigmata, when I don't.

Dieter and Brigitta are deeply moved. Anita approaches them.

Anita Would you like a little dip?

Dieter We're going to go.

Anita What?

Brigitta Sorry.

Peter You're going?

Brigitta Yes.

Anita Is something the matter?

Dieter No . . .

Brigitta We just . . .

Anita Do you two know each other?

86

Dieter No.

Brigitta But it's as if . . .

Dieter (*intimately*) When you find out about me . . .

Brigitta I'll accept everything. Everything you are.

He draws closer.

Please be true.

They kiss. They prepare to leave. The others are staring at them, flabbergasted.

(*to Anita*) Thank you.

Peter Wait! You can't just go!

Dieter Why not?

Peter It's not fair!

They leave.

Why wasn't she like that with me?!

Rita Because you're a creep.

Anita Now, let's not have any nasties, OK? If you don't get on, that's fine. It's best just to call it a day and start again with someone else.

Peter (*to Rita*) Don't you dare speak to me like that.

Rita What's the matter? I thought we were getting on great.

Peter You just called me a creep!

Rita I like creeps. I feel a strong attraction towards them.

Peter *What?*

Anita Peter, why don't you go home and I'll find you someone more suitable in the morning?

Rita Seriously, I'm fascinated. I want to know more about your terrapin.

Peter (*taking the challenge*) I lied about the terrapin. It's a female.

Rita Does it have a name?

Peter Wanda.

Rita Do you mistreat it?

Peter Sometimes.

Rita How?

Peter I put my ex-wife's hairdryer on it.

Rita That's disgusting.

Anita Would you two knock it off?

Peter What else do you find disgusting about me?

Rita Where do you want me to start?

Peter I think you should buy me dinner. I think it's the least you could do after all your lies and insults.

Rita I'll buy the first round of drinks. You buy the dinner.

Anita Rita!

Rita And if you're lucky, I'll throw it over you.

Peter That's exactly what I'd expect.

Anita Rita, stop it.

Rita Why should I?

Anita Peter, I'm really sorry. I had serious doubts about inviting her here tonight. She's extremely unstable and we've had trouble with her before.

Peter That's fine.

Anita She's not what you're looking for, believe me.

Peter I'm looking for an unstable, lapdancing stigmatic.

Rita And I'm looking for a creep with pets.

Anita (*to Rita*) You're going too far!

Rita (*to Peter*) Get out. Now. And dinner's going to be expensive.

Peter You'll pay. One way or the other, you'll pay.

Peter goes. Rita is putting on her coat.

Anita Are you serious?

Rita You know how to stop me.

Anita You're going to go with him, just to get back at me?

Rita Say it.

Anita (*pause*) . . . You can't blackmail me into saying something like that.

Rita Right. See you then.

Anita He's a nut! What if he tries to kill you?

Rita On your head be it. (*She's almost gone.*)

Anita Rita! (*Rita stops. Hopes.*) They fell for each other . . . right before our eyes. Two people just fell . . . I've never seen that before in my life.

Rita (*bitterly disappointed*) It won't last, will it?

Rita goes. Anita is alone.

Anita They fell in l . . . l-l-l-l . . . Rita, I l-l-l – I l-l-l-l-l – I l-l-l –

Anita is in tears. The office disappears. Open land.
Dieter and Brigitta enter.

Dieter Here.

Brigitta You.

Dieter Now.

Brigitta This . . .

They kiss.

Blackout.